MongoDB and Python

Niall O'Higgins

O'REILLY®

Beijing · Cambridge · Farnham · Köln · Sebastopol · Tokyo

MongoDB and Python
by Niall O'Higgins

Published by O'Reilly Media, Inc., 1005 Gravenstein Highway North, Sebastopol, CA 95472.

O'Reilly books may be purchased for educational, business, or sales promotional use. Online editions are also available for most titles (*http://my.safaribooksonline.com*). For more information, contact our corporate/institutional sales department: (800) 998-9938 or *corporate@oreilly.com*.

Editors: Mike Loukides and Shawn Wallace	**Cover Designer:** Karen Montgomery
Production Editor: Jasmine Perez	**Interior Designer:** David Futato
Proofreader: O'Reilly Production Services	**Illustrator:** Robert Romano

ISBN: 978-1-449-31037-0

[LSI]

1315837541

Table of Contents

Preface

I've been building production database-driven applications for about 10 years. I've worked with most of the usual relational databases (MSSQL Server, MySQL, PostgreSQL) and with some very interesting nonrelational databases (Freebase.com's Graphd/MQL, Berkeley DB, MongoDB). MongoDB is at this point the system I enjoy working with the most, and choose for most projects. It sits somewhere at a crossroads between the performance and pragmatism of a relational system and the flexibility and expressiveness of a semantic web database. It has been central to my success in building some quite complicated systems in a short period of time.

I hope that after reading this book you will find MongoDB to be a pleasant database to work with, and one which doesn't get in the way between you and the application you wish to build.

Conventions Used in This Book

The following typographical conventions are used in this book:

Italic
> Indicates new terms, URLs, email addresses, filenames, and file extensions.

`Constant width`
> Used for program listings, as well as within paragraphs to refer to program elements such as variable or function names, databases, data types, environment variables, statements, and keywords.

`Constant width bold`
> Shows commands or other text that should be typed literally by the user.

`Constant width italic`
> Shows text that should be replaced with user-supplied values or by values determined by context.

This icon signifies a tip, suggestion, or general note.

 This icon indicates a warning or caution.

Using Code Examples

This book is here to help you get your job done. In general, you may use the code in this book in your programs and documentation. You do not need to contact us for permission unless you're reproducing a significant portion of the code. For example, writing a program that uses several chunks of code from this book does not require permission. Selling or distributing a CD-ROM of examples from O'Reilly books does require permission. Answering a question by citing this book and quoting example code does not require permission. Incorporating a significant amount of example code from this book into your product's documentation does require permission.

We appreciate, but do not require, attribution. An attribution usually includes the title, author, publisher, and ISBN. For example: "*MongoDB and Python* by Niall O'Higgins. Copyright 2011 O'Reilly Media Inc., 978-1-449-31037-0."

If you feel your use of code examples falls outside fair use or the permission given above, feel free to contact us at *permissions@oreilly.com*.

Safari® Books Online

 Safari Books Online is an on-demand digital library that lets you easily search over 7,500 technology and creative reference books and videos to find the answers you need quickly.

With a subscription, you can read any page and watch any video from our library online. Read books on your cell phone and mobile devices. Access new titles before they are available for print, and get exclusive access to manuscripts in development and post feedback for the authors. Copy and paste code samples, organize your favorites, download chapters, bookmark key sections, create notes, print out pages, and benefit from tons of other time-saving features.

O'Reilly Media has uploaded this book to the Safari Books Online service. To have full digital access to this book and others on similar topics from O'Reilly and other publishers, sign up for free at *http://my.safaribooksonline.com*.

How to Contact Us

Please address comments and questions concerning this book to the publisher:

O'Reilly Media, Inc.
1005 Gravenstein Highway North
Sebastopol, CA 95472
800-998-9938 (in the United States or Canada)
707-829-0515 (international or local)
707-829-0104 (fax)

We have a web page for this book, where we list errata, examples, and any additional information. You can access this page at:

http://www.oreilly.com/catalog/0636920021513

To comment or ask technical questions about this book, send email to:

bookquestions@oreilly.com

For more information about our books, courses, conferences, and news, see our website at *http://www.oreilly.com*.

Find us on Facebook: *http://facebook.com/oreilly*

Follow us on Twitter: *http://twitter.com/oreillymedia*

Watch us on YouTube: *http://www.youtube.com/oreillymedia*

Acknowledgments

I would like to thank Ariel Backenroth, Aseem Mohanty and Eugene Ciurana for giving detailed feedback on the first draft of this book. I would also like to thank the O'Reilly team for making it a great pleasure to write the book. Of course, thanks to all the people at 10gen without whom MongoDB would not exist and this book would not have been possible.

## CHAPTER 1

Getting Started

Introduction

First released in 2009, MongoDB is relatively new on the database scene compared to contemporary giants like Oracle which trace their first releases to the 1970's. As a document-oriented database generally grouped into the NoSQL category, it stands out among distributed key value stores, Amazon Dynamo clones and Google BigTable re-implementations. With a focus on rich operator support and high performance Online Transaction Processing (OLTP), MongoDB is in many ways closer to MySQL than to batch-oriented databases like HBase.

The key differences between MongoDB's document-oriented approach and a traditional relational database are:

1. MongoDB does not support joins.

2. MongoDB does not support transactions. It does have some support for atomic operations, however.

3. MongoDB schemas are flexible. Not all documents in a collection must adhere to the same schema.

1 and 2 are a direct result of the huge difficulties in making these features scale across a large distributed system while maintaining acceptable performance. They are trade-offs made in order to allow for horizontal scalability. Although MongoDB lacks joins, it does introduce some alternative capabilites, e.g. embedding, which can be used to solve many of the same data modeling problems as joins. Of course, even if embedding doesn't quite work, you can always perform your join in application code, by making multiple queries.

The lack of transactions can be painful at times, but fortunately MongoDB supports a fairly decent set of atomic operations. From the basic atomic increment and decrement operators to the richer "findAndModify", which is essentially an atomic read-modify-write operator.

It turns out that a flexible schema can be very beneficial, especially when you expect to be iterating quickly. While up front schema design—as used in the relational model—has its place, there is often a heavy cost in terms of maintenance. Handling schema updates in the relational world is of course doable, but comes with a price.

In MongoDB, you can add new properties at any time, dynamically, without having to worry about ALTER TABLE statements that can take hours to run and complicated data migration scripts. However, this approach does come with its own tradeoffs. For example, type enforcement must be carefully handled by the application code. Custom document versioning might be desirable to avoid large conditional blocks to handle heterogeneous documents in the same collection.

The dynamic nature of MongoDB lends itself quite naturally to working with a dynamic language such as Python. The tradeoffs between a dynamically typed language such as Python and a statically typed language such as Java in many respects mirror the tradeoffs between the flexible, document-oriented model of MongoDB and the up-front and statically typed schema definition of SQL databases.

Python allows you to express MongoDB documents and queries natively, through the use of existing language features like nested dictionaries and lists. If you have worked with JSON in Python, you will immediately be comfortable with MongoDB documents and queries.

For these reasons, MongoDB and Python make a powerful combination for rapid, iterative development of horizontally scalable backend applications. For the vast majority of modern Web and mobile applications, we believe MongoDB is likely a better fit than RDBMS technology.

Finding Reference Documentation

MongoDB, Python, 10gen's PyMongo driver and each of the Web frameworks mentioned in this book all have good reference documentation online.

For MongoDB, we would strongly suggest bookmarking and at least skimming over the official MongoDB manual which is available in a few different formats and constantly updated at *http://www.mongodb.org/display/DOCS/Manual*. While the manual describes the JavaScript interface via the mongo console utility as opposed to the Python interface, most of the code snippets should be easily understood by a Python programmer and more-or-less portable to PyMongo, albeit sometimes with a little bit of work. Furthermore, the MongoDB manual goes into greater depth on certain advanced and technical implementation and database administration topics than is possible in this book.

For the Python language and standard library, you can use the `help()` function in the interpreter or the `pydoc` tool on the command line to get API documentation for any methods or modules. For example:

```
pydoc string
```

The latest Python language and API documentation is also available for online browsing at *http://docs.python.org/*.

10gen's PyMongo driver has API documentation available online to go with each release. You can find this at *http://api.mongodb.org/python/*. Additionally, once you have the PyMongo driver package installed on your system, a summary version of the API documentation should be available to you in the Python interpreter via the `help()` function. Due to an issue with the `virtualenv` tool mentioned in the next section, "pydoc" does not work inside a virtual environment. You must instead run `python -m pydoc pymongo`.

Installing MongoDB

For the purposes of development, it is recommended to run a MongoDB server on your local machine. This will permit you to iterate quickly and try new things without fear of destroying a production database. Additionally, you will be able to develop with MongoDB even without an Internet connection.

Depending on your operating system, you may have multiple options for how to install MongoDB locally.

Most modern UNIX-like systems will have a version of MongoDB available in their package management system. This includes FreeBSD, Debian, Ubuntu, Fedora, CentOS and ArchLinux. Installing one of these packages is likely the most convenient approach, although the version of MongoDB provided by your packaging vendor may lag behind the latest release from 10gen. For local development, as long as you have the latest major release, you are probably fine.

10gen also provides their own MongoDB packages for many systems which they update very quickly on each release. These can be a little more work to get installed but ensure you are running the latest-and-greatest. After the initial setup, they are typically trivial to keep up-to-date. For a production deployment, where you likely want to be able to update to the most recent stable MongoDB version with a minimum of hassle, this option probably makes the most sense.

In addition to the system package versions of MongoDB, 10gen provide binary zip and tar archives. These are independent of your system package manager and are provided in both 32-bit and 64-bit flavours for OS X, Windows, Linux and Solaris. 10gen also provide statically-built binary distributions of this kind for Linux, which may be your best option if you are stuck on an older, legacy Linux system lacking the modern libc and other library versions. Also, if you are on OS X, Windows or Solaris, these are probably your best bet.

Finally, you can always build your own binaries from the source code. Unless you need to make modifications to MongoDB internals yourself, this method is best avoided due to the time and complexity involved.

In the interests of simplicity, we will provide the commands required to install a stable version of MongoDB using the system package manager of the most common UNIX-like operating systems. This is the easiest method, assuming you are on one of these platforms. For Mac OS X and Windows, we provide instructions to install the binary packages from 10gen.

Ubuntu / Debian:

```
sudo apt-get update; sudo apt-get install mongodb
```

Fedora:

```
sudo yum install mongo-stable-server
```

FreeBSD:

```
sudo pkg_add -r mongodb
```

Windows:

Go to *http://www.mongodb.org* and download the latest production release zip file for Windows—choosing 32-bit or 64-bit depending on your system. Extract the contents of the zipfile to a location like C:\mongodb and add the bin directory to your PATH.

Mac OS X:

Go to *http://www.mongodb.org* and download the latest production release compressed tar file for OS X—choosing 32-bit or 64-bit depending on your system. Extract the contents to a location like /usr/local/ or /opt and add the bin directory to your $PATH. For exmaple:

```
cd /tmp
wget http://fastdl.mongodb.org/osx/mongodb-osx-x86_64-1.8.3-rc1.tgz
tar xfz mongodb-osx-x86_64-1.8.3-rc1.tgz
sudo mkdir /usr/local/mongodb
sudo cp -r mongodb-osx-x86_64-1.8.3-rc1/bin /usr/local/mongodb/
export PATH=$PATH:/usr/local/mongodb/bin
```

Running MongoDB

On some platforms—such as Ubuntu—the package manager will automatically start the mongod daemon for you, and ensure it starts on boot also. On others, such as Mac OS X, you must write your own script to start it, and manually integrate with launchd so that it starts on system boot.

Note that before you can start MongoDB, its data and log directories must exist.

If you wish to have MongoDB start automatically on boot on Windows, 10gen have a document describing how to set this up at *http://www.mongodb.org/display/DOCS/Windows+Service*

To have MongoDB start automatically on boot under Mac OS X, first you will need a plist file. Save the following (changing db and log paths appropriately) to /Library/LaunchDaemons/org.mongodb.mongod.plist:

```xml
<?xml version="1.0" encoding="UTF-8"?>
<!DOCTYPE plist PUBLIC "-//Apple//DTD PLIST 1.0//EN" "http://www.apple.com/DTDs/
PropertyList-1.0.dtd">
<plist version="1.0">
<dict>
        <key>RunAtLoad</key>
        <true/>
        <key>Label</key>
        <string>org.mongo.mongod</string>
        <key>ProgramArguments</key>
        <array>
                <string>/usr/local/mongodb/bin/mongod</string>
                <string>--dbpath</string>
```

```
            <string>/usr/local/mongodb/data/</string>
            <string>--logpath</string>
            <string>/usr/local/mongodb/log/mongodb.log</string>
        </array>
    </dict>
</plist>
```

Next run the following commands to activate the startup script with launchd:

```
sudo launchctl load /Library/LaunchDaemons/org.mongodb.mongod.plist
sudo launchctl start org.mongodb.mongod
```

A quick way to test whether there is a MongoDB instance already running on your local machine is to type mongo at the command-line. This will start the MongoDB admin console, which attempts to connect to a database server running on the default port (27017).

In any case, you can always start MongoDB manually from the command-line. This is a useful thing to be familiar with in case you ever want to test features such as replica sets or sharding by running multiple mongod instances on your local machine.

Assuming the mongod binary is in your $PATH, run:

```
mongod --logpath <path/to/mongo.logfile> --port <port to listen on> --dbpath <path/to/
data directory>
```

Setting up a Python Environment with MongoDB

In order to be able to connect to MongoDB with Python, you need to install the Py-Mongo driver package. In Python, the best practice is to create what is known as a "virtual environment" in which to install your packages. This isolates them cleanly from any "system" packages you have installed and yields the added bonus of not requiring root privileges to install additional Python packages. The tool to create a "virtual environment" is called virtualenv.

There are two approaches to installing the virtualenv tool on your system—manually and via your system package management tool. Most modern UNIX-like systems will have the virtualenv tool in their package repositories. For example, on Mac OS X with Mac Ports, you can run sudo port install py27-virtualenv to install virtualenv for Python 2.7. On Ubuntu you can run sudo apt-get install python-virtualenv. Refer to the documentation for your OS to learn how to install it on your specific platform.

In case you are unable or simply don't want to use your system's package manager, you can always install it yourself, by hand. In order to manually install it, you must have the Python setuptools package. You may already have setuptools on your system. You can test this by running python -c import setuptools on the command line. If nothing is printed and you are simply returned to the prompt, you don't need to do anything. If an ImportError is raised, you need to install setuptools.

To manually install setuptools, first download the file *http://peak.telecommunity.com/dist/ez_setup.py*

Then run `python ez_setup.py` as root.

For Windows, first download and install the latest Python 2.7.x package from *http://www.python.org*. Once you have installed Python, download and install the Windows setuptools installer package from *http://pypi.python.org/pypi/setuptools/*. After installing Python 2.7 and setuptools, you will have the easy_install tool available on your machine in the Python scripts directory—default is C:\Python27\Scripts\.

Once you have setuptools installed on your system, run `easy_install virtualenv` as root.

Now that you have the "virtualenv" tool available on your machine, you can create your first virtual Python environment. You can do this by executing the command `virtualenv --no-site-packages myenv`. You do not need—and indeed should not want—to run this command with root privileges. This will create a virtual environment in the directory "myenv". The --no-site-packages option to the "virtualenv" utility instructs it to create a clean Python environment, isolated from any existing packages installed in the system.

You are now ready to install the PyMongo driver.

With the "myenv" directory as your working directory (i.e. after "cd myenv"), simply execute `bin/easy_install pymongo`. This will install the latest stable version of PyMongo into your virtual Python environment. To verify that this worked successfully, execute the command `bin/python -c import pymongo`, making sure that the "myenv" directory is still your working directory, as with the previous command.

Assuming Python did not raise an ImportError, you now have a Python virtualenv with the PyMongo driver correctly installed and are ready to connect to MongoDB and start issuing queries!

## CHAPTER 2

Reading and Writing to MongoDB with Python

MongoDB is a document-oriented database. This is different from a relational database in two significant ways. Firstly, not all entries must adhere to the same schema. Secondly you can embed entries inside of one another. Despite these major differences, there are analogs to SQL concepts in MongoDB. A logical group of entries in a SQL database is termed a table. In MongoDB, the analogous term is a collection. A single entry in a SQL databse is termed a row. In MongoDB, the analog is a document.

Table 2-1. Comparison of SQL/RDBMS and MongoDB Concepts and Terms

Concept	SQL	MongoDB
One User	One Row	One Document
All Users	Users Table	Users Collection
One Username Per User (1-to-1)	Username Column	Username Property
Many Emails Per User (1-to-many)	SQL JOIN with Emails Table	Embed relevant email doc in User Document
Many Items Owned by Many Users (many-to-many)	SQL JOIN with Items Table	Programmatically Join with Items Collection

Hence, in MongoDB, you are mostly operating on documents and collections of documents. If you are familiar with JSON, a MongoDB document is essentially a JSON document with a few extra features. From a Python perspective, it is a Python dictionary.

Consider the following example of a user document with a username, first name, surname, date of birth, email address and score:

```
from datetime import datetime
user_doc = {
    "username" : "janedoe",
    "firstname" : "Jane",
```

```
        "surname" : "Doe",
        "dateofbirth" : datetime(1974, 4, 12),
        "email" : "janedoe74@example.com",
        "score" : 0
    }
```

As you can see, this is a native Python object. Unlike SQL, there is no special syntax to deal with. The PyMongo driver transparently supports Python datetime objects. This is very convenient when working with datetime instances—the driver will transparently marshall the values for you in both reads and writes. You should never have to write datetime conversion code yourself.

Instead of grouping things inside of tables, as in SQL, MongoDB groups them in collections. Like SQL tables, MongoDB collections can have indexes on particular document properties for faster lookups and you can read and write to them using complex query predicates. Unlike SQL tables, documents in a MongoDB collection do not all have to conform to the same schema.

Returning to our user example above, such documents would be logically grouped in a "users" collection.

Connecting to MongoDB with Python

The PyMongo driver makes connecting to a MongoDB database quite straight forward. Furthermore, the driver supports some nice features right out of the box, such as connection pooling and automatic reconnect on failure (when working with a replicated setup). If you are familiar with more traditional RDBMS/SQL systems—for example MySQL—you are likely used to having to deploy additional software, or possibly even write your own, to handle connection pooling and automatic reconnect. 10gen very thoughtfully relieved us of the need to worry about these details when working with MongoDB and the PyMongo driver. This takes a lot of the headache out of running a production MongoDB-based system.

You instantiate a Connection object with the necessary parameters. By default, the Connection object will connect to a MongoDB server on localhost at port 27017. To be explicit, we'll pass those parameters along in our example:

```
""" An example of how to connect to MongoDB """
import sys

from pymongo import Connection
from pymongo.errors import ConnectionFailure

def main():
    """ Connect to MongoDB """
    try:
        c = Connection(host="localhost", port=27017)
        print "Connected successfully"
    except ConnectionFailure, e:
        sys.stderr.write("Could not connect to MongoDB: %s" % e)
```

```
        sys.exit(1)

    if __name__ == "__main__":
        main()
```

As you can see, a ConnectionFailure exception can be thrown by Connection instantiation. It is usually a good idea to handle this exception and output something informative to your users.

Getting a Database Handle

Connection objects themselves are not all that frequently used when working with MongoDB in Python. Typically you create one once, and then forget about it. This is because most of the real interaction happens with Database and Collection objects. Connection objects are just a way to get a handle on your first Databse object. In fact, even if you lose reference to the Connection object, you can always get it back because Database objects have a reference to the Connection object.

Getting a Database object is easy once you have a Connection instance. You simply need to know the name of the database, and the username and password to access it if you are using authorization on it.

```
""" An example of how to get a Python handle to a MongoDB database """
import sys

from pymongo import Connection
from pymongo.errors import ConnectionFailure

def main():
    """ Connect to MongoDB """
    try:
        c = Connection(host="localhost", port=27017)
    except ConnectionFailure, e:
        sys.stderr.write("Could not connect to MongoDB: %s" % e)
        sys.exit(1)
    # Get a Database handle to a database named "mydb"
    dbh = c["mydb"]

    # Demonstrate the db.connection property to retrieve a reference to the
    # Connection object should it go out of scope. In most cases, keeping a
    # reference to the Database object for the lifetime of your program should
    # be sufficient.

    assert dbh.connection == c
    print "Successfully set up a database handle"

if __name__ == "__main__":
    main()
```

Inserting a Document into a Collection

Once you have a handle to your database, you can begin inserting data. Let us imagine we have a collection called "users", containing all the users of our game. Each user has a username, a first name, surname, date of birth, email address and a score. We want to add a new user:

```python
""" An example of how to insert a document """
import sys

from datetime import datetime
from pymongo import Connection
from pymongo.errors import ConnectionFailure

def main():
    try:
        c = Connection(host="localhost", port=27017)
    except ConnectionFailure, e:
        sys.stderr.write("Could not connect to MongoDB: %s" % e)
        sys.exit(1)
    dbh = c["mydb"]
    assert dbh.connection == c
    user_doc = {
        "username" : "janedoe",
        "firstname" : "Jane",
        "surname" : "Doe",
        "dateofbirth" : datetime(1974, 4, 12),
        "email" : "janedoe74@example.com",
        "score" : 0
    }

    dbh.users.insert(user_doc, safe=True)
    print "Successfully inserted document: %s" % user_doc

if __name__ == "__main__":
    main()
```

Note that we don't have to tell MongoDB to create our collection "users" before we insert to it. Collections are created lazily in MongoDB, whenever you access them. This has the advantage of being very lightweight, but can occasionally cause problems due to typos. These can be hard to track down unless you have good test coverage. For example, imagine you accidentally typed:

```python
# dbh.usrs is a typo, we mean dbh.users!  Unlike an RDBMS, MongoDB won't
# protect you from this class of mistake.
dbh.usrs.insert(user_doc)
```

The code would execute correctly and no errors would be thrown. You might be left scratching your head wondering why your user document isn't there. We recommend being extra vigilant to double check your spelling when addressing collections. Good test coverage can also help find bugs of this sort.

Another feature of MongoDB inserts to be aware of is primary key auto-generation. In MongoDB, the `_id` property on a document is treated specially. It is considered to be the primary key for that document, and is expected to be unique unless the collection has been explcitly created without an index on `_id`. By default, if no `_id` property is present in a document you insert, MongoDB will generate one itself. When MongoDB generates an `_id` property itself, it uses the type ObjectId. A MongoDB ObjectId is a 96-bit value which is expected to have a very high probability of being unique when created. It can be considered similar in purpose to a UUID object as defined by RFC 4122. MongoDB ObjectIds have the nice property of being almost-certainly-unique upon generation, hence no central coordination is required.

This contrasts sharply with the common RDBMS idiom of using auto-increment primary keys. Guaranteeing that an auto-increment key is not already in use usually requires consulting some centralized system. When the intention is to provide a horizontally scalable, de-centralized and fault-tolerant database—as is the case with MongoDB—auto-increment keys represent an ugly bottleneck.

By employing ObjectId as your `_id`, you leave the door open to horizontal scaling via MongoDB's sharding capabilities. While you can in fact supply your own value for the `_id` property if you wish—so long as it is globally unique—this is best avoided unless there is a strong reason to do otherwise. Examples of cases where you may be forced to provide your own `_id` property value include migration from RDBMS systems which utilized the previously-mentioned auto-increment primary key idiom.

Note that an ObjectId can be just as easily generated on the client-side, with PyMongo, as by the server. To generate an ObjectId with PyMongo, you simply instantiate `pymongo.objectid.ObjectId`.

Write to a Collection Safely and Synchronously

By default, the PyMongo driver performs asynchronous writes. Write operations include insert, update, remove and findAndModify.

Asynchronous writes are unsafe in the sense that they are not checked for errors and so execution of your program could continue without any guarantees of the write having completed successfully. While asynchronous writes improve performance by not blocking execution, they can easily lead to nasty race conditions and other nefarious data integrity bugs. For this reason, we recommend you almost always use safe, synchronous, blocking writes. It seems rare in practice to have truly "fire-and-forget" writes where there are aboslutely no consequences for failures. That being said, one common example where asynchronous writes may make sense is when you are writing non-critical logs or analytics data to MongoDB from your application.

Unless you are certain you don't need synchronous writes, we recommend that you pass the "safe=True" keyword argument to inserts, updates, removes and findAndModify operations:

```
# safe=True ensures that your write
# will succeed or an exception will be thrown
dbh.users.insert(user_doc, safe=True)
```

Guaranteeing Writes to Multiple Database Nodes

The term node refers to a single instance of the MongoDB daemon process. Typically there is a single MongoDB node per machine, but for testing or development cases you can run multiple nodes on one machine.

Replica Set is the MongoDB term for the database's enhanced master-slave replication configuration. This is similar to the traditional master-slave replication you find in RDBMS such as MySQL and PostgreSQL in that a single node handles writes at a given time. In MongoDB master selection is determined by an election protocol and during failover a slave is automatically promoted to master without requiring operator intervention. Furthermore, the PyMongo driver is Replica Set-aware and performs automatic reconnect on failure to the new master. MongoDB Replica Sets, therefore, represent a master-slave replication configuration with excellent failure handling out of the box. For anyone who has had to manually recover from a MySQL master failure in a production environment, this feature is a welcome relief.

By default, MongoDB will return success for your write operation once it has been written to a single node in a Replica Set.

However, for added safety in case of failure, you may wish your write to be committed to two or more replicas before returning success. This can help ensure that in case of catastrophic failure, at least one of the nodes in the Replica Set will have your write.

PyMongo makes it easy to specify how many nodes you would like your write to be replicated to before returning success. You simply set a parameter named "w" to the number of servers in each write method call.

For example:

```
# w=2 means the write will not succeed until it has
# been written to at least 2 servers in a replica set.
dbh.users.insert(user_doc, w=2)
```

Note that passing any value of "w" to a write method in PyMongo implies setting "safe=True" also.

Introduction to MongoDB Query Language

MongoDB queries are represented as a JSON-like structure, just like documents. To build a query, you specify a document with properties you wish the results to match. MongoDB treats each property as having an implicit boolean AND. It natively supports boolean OR queries, but you must use a special operator ($or) to achieve it. In addition to exact matches, MongoDB has operators for greater than, less than, etc.

Sample query document to match all documents in the users collection with firstname "jane":

```
q  = {
    "firstname" : "jane"
}
```

If we wanted to retrieve all documents with firstname "jane" AND surname "doe", we would write:

```
q = {
    "firstname" : "jane",
    "surname" : "doe"
}
```

If we wanted to retrieve all documents with a score value of greater than 0, we would write:

```
q = {
    "score" : { "$gt" : 0 }
}
```

Notice the use of the special "$gt" operator. The MongoDB query language provides a number of such operators, enabling you to build quite complex queries.

See the section on MongoDB Query Operators for details.

Reading, Counting, and Sorting Documents in a Collection

In many situations, you only want to retrieve a single document from a collection. This is especially true when documents in your collection are unique on some property. A good example of this is a users collection, where each username is guaranteed unique.

```
# Assuming we already have a database handle in scope named dbh
# find a single document with the username "janedoe".
user_doc = dbh.users.find_one({"username" : "janedoe"})
if not user_doc:
    print "no document found for username janedoe"
```

Notice that find_one() will return None if no document is found.

Now imagine you wish to find all documents in the users collection which have a firstname property set to "jane" and print out their email addresses. MongoDB will return a Cursor object for us, to stream the results. PyMongo handles result streaming as you iterate, so if you have a huge number of results they are not all stored in memory at once.

```
# Assuming we already have a database handle in scope named dbh
# find all documents with the firstname "jane".
# Then iterate through them and print out the email address.
users = dbh.users.find({"firstname":"jane"})
for user in users:
    print user.get("email")
```

Notice in the above example that we use the Python dict class' get method. If we were certain that every single result document contained the "email" property, we could have used dictionary access instead.

```
for user in users:
    print user["email"]
```

If you only wish to retrieve a subset of the properties from each document in a collection during a read, you can pass those as a dictionary via an additional parameter. For example, suppose that you only wish to retrieve the email address for each user with firstname "jane":

```
# Only retrieve the "email" field from each matching document.
users = dbh.users.find({"firstname":"jane"}, {"email":1})
for user in users:
    print user.get("email")
```

If you are retrieving a large result set, requesting only the properties you need can reduce network and decoding overhead, potentially increasing performance.

Sometimes you are not so interested in the query results themselves, but are looking to find the size of the result set for a given query. A common example is an analytics situation where you want a count of how many documents are in your users' collections. MonogDB supports efficient server-side counting of result sets with the count() method on Cursor objects:

```
# Find out how many documents are in users collection, efficiently
userscount = dbh.users.find().count()
print "There are %d documents in users collection" % userscount
```

MongoDB can also perform result sorting for you on the server-side. Especially if you are sorting results on a property which has an index, it can sort these far more efficiently than your client program can. PyMongo Cursor objects have a sort() method which takes a Python 2-tuple comprising the property to sort on, and the direction. The Py-Mongo sort() method is analogous to the SQL ORDER BY statement. Direction can either be pymongo.ASCENDING or pymongo.DESCENDING. For example:

```
# Return all user with firstname "jane" sorted
# in descending order by birthdate (ie youngest first)
users = dbh.users.find(
    {"firstname":"jane"}).sort(("dateofbirth", pymongo.DESCENDING))
for user in users:
    print user.get("email")
```

In addition to the sort() method on the PyMongo Cursor object, you may also pass sort instructions to the find() and find_one() methods on the PyMongo Collection object. Using this facility, the above example may be rewritten as:

```
# Return all user with firstname "jane" sorted
# in descending order by birthdate (ie youngest first)
users = dbh.users.find({"firstname":"jane"},
    sort=[("dateofbirth", pymongo.DESCENDING)])
for user in users:
    print user.get("email")
```

Another situation you may encounter—especially when you have large result sets—is that you wish to only fetch a limited number of results. This is frequently combined with server-side sorting of results. For example, imagine you are generating a high score table which displays only the top ten scores. PyMongo Cursor objects have a limit() method which enables this. The limit() method is analogous to the SQL LIMIT statement.

```
# Return at most 10 users sorted by score in descending order
# This may be used as a "top 10 users highscore table"
users = dbh.users.find().sort(("score", pymongo.DESCENDING)).limit(10)
for user in users:
    print user.get("username"), user.get("score", 0)
```

If you know in advance that you only need a limited number of results from a query, using limit() can yield a performance benefit. This is because it may greatly reduce the size of the results data which must be sent by MongoDB. Note that a limit of 0 is equivalent to no limit.

Additionally, MongoDB can support skipping to a specific offset in a result set through the Cursor.skip() method provided by PyMongo. When used with limit() this enables result pagination which is frequently used by clients when allowing end-users to browse very large result sets. skip() is analogous to the SQL OFFSET statement. For example, imagine a Web application which displays 20 users per page, sorted alphabetically by surname , and needs to fetch the data to build the second page of results for a user. The query used by the Web application might look like this:

```
# Return at most 20 users sorted by name,
# skipping the first 20 results in the set
users = dbh.users.find().sort(
    ("surname", pymongo.ASCENDING)).limit(20).skip(20)
```

Finally, when traversing very large result sets, where the underlying documents may be modified by other programs at the same time, you may wish to use MongoDB's Snapshot Mode. Imagine a busy site with hundreds of thousands of users. You are developing an analytics program to count users and build various statistics about usage patterns and so on. However, this analytics program is intended to run against the live, production database. Since this is such a busy site, real users are frequently performing actions on the site which may result in modifications to their corresponding user documents—while your analytics program is running. Due to quirks in MongoDB's cursoring mechanism, in this kind of situation your program could easily see duplicates in your query result set. Duplicate data could throw off the accuracy of your analysis program, and so it is best avoided. This is where Snapshot Mode comes in.

MongoDB's Snapshot Mode guarantees that documents which are modified during the lifetime of a query are returned only once in a result set. In other words, duplicates are eliminated, and you should not have to worry about them.

 However, Snapshot Mode does have some limitations. Snapshot Mode cannot be used with sorting, nor can it be used with an index on any property other than _id.

To use Snapshot Mode with PyMongo, simply pass "snapshot=True" as a parameter to the find() method:

```
# Traverse the entire users collection, employing Snapshot Mode
# to eliminate potential duplicate results.
for user in dbh.users.find(snapshot=True):
    print user.get("username"), user.get("score", 0)
```

Updating Documents in a Collection

Update queries in MongoDB consist of two parts: a document spec which informs the database of the set of documents to be updated, and the update document itself.

The first part, the document spec, is the same as the query document which you use with find() or find_one().

The second part, the update document, can be used in two ways. The simplest is to supply the full document which will replace the matched document in the collection. For example, suppose you had the following document in your users collection:

```
user_doc = {
    "username" : "janedoe",
    "firstname" : "Jane",
    "surname" : "Doe",
    "dateofbirth" : datetime(1974, 4, 12),
    "email" : "janedoe74@example.com",
    "score" : 0
}
```

Now let's say you wish to update the document with username "janedoe" to change the email address to "janedoe74@example2.com". We build a completely new document which is identical to the original, except for the new email address.

```
# first query to get a copy of the current document
import copy
old_user_doc = dbh.users.find_one({"username":"janedoe"})
new_user_doc = copy.deepcopy(old_user_doc)
# modify the copy to change the email address
new_user_doc["email"] = "janedoe74@example2.com"
# run the update query
# replace the matched document with the contents of new_user_doc
dbh.users.update({"username":"janedoe"}, new_user_doc, safe=True)
```

Building the whole replacement document can be cumbersome, and worse, can introduce race conditions. Imagine you want to increment the score property of the "janedoe" user. In order to achieve this with the replacement approach, you would have to first fetch the document, modify it with the incremented score, then write it back to the database. With that approach, you could easily lose other score changes if something else were to update the score in between you reading and writing it.

In order to solve this problem, the update document supports an additional set of MongoDB operators called "update modifiers". These update modifiers include operators such as atomic increment/decrement, atomic list push/pop and so on. It is very helpful to be aware of which update modifiers are available and what they can do when designing your application. Many of these will be described in their own recipes throughout this book.

To illustrate usage of "update modifiers", let's return to our original example of changing only the email address of the document with username "janedoe". We can use the $set update modifier in our update document to avoid having to query before updating. $set changes the value of an individual property or a group of properties to whatever you specify.

```
# run the update query, using the $set update modifier.
# we do not need to know the current contents of the document
# with this approach, and so avoid an initial query and
# potential race condition.
dbh.users.update({"username":"janedoe"},
    {"$set":{"email":"janedoe74@example2.com"}}, safe=True)
```

You can also set multiple properties at once using the $set update modifier:

```
# update the email address and the score at the same time
# using $set in a single write.
dbh.users.update({"username":"janedoe"},
    {"$set":{"email":"janedoe74@example2.com", "score":1}}, safe=True)
```

 At the time of writing, the PyMongo driver, even if you specify a document spec to the update method which matches multiple documents in a collection, only applies the update to the first document matched.

In other words, even if you believe your update document spec matches every single document in the collection, your update will only write to one of those documents.

For example, let us imagine we wish to set a flag on every document in our users collection which has a score of 0:

```
# even if every document in your collection has a score of 0,
# only the first matched document will have its "flagged" property set to True.
dbh.users.update({"score":0},{"$set":{"flagged":True}}, safe=True)
```

In order to have your update query write multiple documents, you must pass the "multi=True" parameter to the update method.

```
# once we supply the "multi=True" parameter, all matched documents
# will be updated
dbh.users.update({"score":0},{"$set":{"flagged":True}}, multi=True, safe=True)
```

Although the default value for the multi parameter to the update method is currently False—meaning only the first matched document will be updated—this may change. The PyMongo documentation currently recommends that you explicitly set multi=False if you are relying on this default, to avoid breakage in future. Note that this should only impact you if you are working with a collection where your documents are not unique on the property you are querying on in your document spec.

Deleting Documents from a Collection

If you wish to permanently delete documents from a collection, it is quite easy to do so. The PyMongo Collection object has a remove() method. As with reads and updates, you specify which documents you want to remove by way of a document spec. For example, to delete all documents from the users collection with a score of 1, you would use the following code:

```
# Delete all documents in user collection with score 1
dbh.users.remove({"score":1}, safe=True)
```

Note that the remove() method takes a safe parameter. As mentioned in the earlier section "Write to a Collection Safely and Synchronously", it is recommended to set the safe parameter to True on write methods to ensure the operation has completed. It is also worth noting that remove() will not raise any exception or error if no documents are matched.

Finally, if you wish to delete all documents in a collection, you can pass None as a parameter to `remove()`:

```
# Delete all documents in user collection
dbh.users.remove(None, safe=True)
```

Clearing a collection with `remove()` differs from dropping the collection via `drop_col lection()` in that the indexes will remain intact.

MongoDB Query Operators

As mentioned previously, MongoDB has quite a rich set of query operators and predicates. In Table 2-2 we provide a table with the meaning of each one, along with a sample usage and the SQL equivalent where applicable.

Table 2-2. MongoDB query operators

Operator	Meaning	Example	SQL Equivalent
$gt	Greater Than	"score":{"$gt":0}	>
$lt	Less Than	"score":{"$lt":0}	<
$gte	Greater Than or Equal	"score":{"$gte":0}	>=
$lte	Less Than or Equal	"score":{"$lte":0}	<=
$all	Array Must Contain All	"skills":{"$all":["mongodb","python"]}	N/A
$exists	Property Must Exist	"email":{"$exists":True}	N/A
$mod	Modulo X Equals Y	"seconds":{"$mod":[60,0]}	MOD()
$ne	Not Equals	"seconds":{"$ne":60}	!=
$in	In	"skills":{"$in":["c","c++"]}	IN
$nin	Not In	"skills":{"$nin":["php","ruby","perl"]}	NOT IN
$nor	Nor	"$nor":[{"language":"english"},{"country":"usa"}]	N/A
$or	Or	"$or":[{"language":"english"},{"country":"usa"}]	OR
$size	Array Must Be Of Size	"skills":{"$size":3}	N/A

If you do not fully understand the meaning or purpose of some of these operators immediately do not worry. We shall discuss the practical use of some of the more advanced operators in detail in Chapter 3.

MongoDB Update Modifiers

As mentioned in the section "Updating Documents in a Collection", MongoDB comes with a set of operators for performing atomic modifications on documents.

Table 2-3. MongoDB update modifiers

Modifier	Meaning	Example
$inc	Atomic Increment	"$inc":{"score":1}
$set	Set Property Value	"$set":{"username":"niall"}
$unset	Unset (delete) Property	"$unset":{"username":1}
$push	Atomic Array Append (atom)	"$push":{"emails":"foo@example.com"}
$pushAll	Atomic Array Append (list)	"$pushall":{"emails":["foo@example.com","foo2@example.com"]}
$addToSet	Atomic Append-If-Not-Present	"$addToSet":{"emails":"foo@example.com"}
$pop	Atomic Array Tail Remove	"$pop":{"emails":1}
$pull	Atomic Conditional Array Item Removal	"$pull":{"emails":"foo@example.com"}
$pullAll	Atomic Array Multi Item Removal	"$pullAll":{"emails":["foo@example.com", "foo2@example.com"]}
$rename	Atomic Property Rename	"$rename":{"emails":"old_emails"}

As with the MongoDB query operators listed earlier in this chapter, this table is mostly for your reference. These operators will be introduced in greater detail in Chapter 3.

Common MongoDB and Python Patterns

After some time working with MongoDB and Python to solve different problems, various patterns and best practices begin to emerge. Just as with any programming language and database system, there are established approaches for modeling data along with known methods for answering queries as quickly and efficiently as possible.

While there are myriad sources of such knowledge for traditional RDBM systems like MySQL, there are far fewer resources available for MongoDB. This chapter is an attempt to address this.

A Uniquely Document-Oriented Pattern: Embedding

While the ability of MongoDB documents to contain sub-documents has been mentioned previously in this book, it has not been explored in detail. In fact, embedding is an extremely important modeling technique when working with MongoDB and can have important performance and scalability implications. In particular, embedding can be used to solve many data modeling problems usually solved by a join in traditional RDBMS. Furthermore, embedding is perhaps more intuitive and easier to understand than a join.

What exactly is meant by embedding? In Python terms, when the value of a key in a dictionary is yet another dictionary, we say that you are embedding the latter in the former. For example:

```
my_document = {
    "name":"foo document",
    "data":{"name":"bar document"}
}
```

Here, "data" is a sub-document embedded in the top-level document "my_document".

Embedding sub-documents can be a useful, natural technique to reduce clutter or namespace collisions. For example consider the case where a "user" document should reference Facebook, Twitter and IRC account usernames, passwords and associated details—in addition to storing a "username" property native to your applicaton:

```
user_doc = {
    "username":"foouser",
    "twitter":{
        "username":"footwitter",
        "password":"secret",
        "email":"twitter@example.com"
    },
    "facebook":{
        "username":"foofacebook",
        "password":"secret",
        "email":"facebook@example.com"
    },
    "irc":{
        "username":"fooirc",
        "password":"secret",
    }
}
```

 Note that in MongoDB documents—just as in Python dictionaries—property names (a.k.a. keys) are unique. In other words, a single document can only ever have one "username" property. This rule also applies to properties in embedded sub-documents. This uniqueness constraint can actually be exploited and enable some useful patterns. Specifically, see the section titled "Fast Accounting Pattern".

Of course, embedded sub-documents can be queried against just like their top-level counterparts. For example, it would be completely legal to attempt to query for the above document in a collection called "users" with the following statement:

```
user_doc = dbh.users.find_one({"facebook.username":"foofacebook"})
```

As you can see, the dot (".") is used to denote keys in an embedded sub-document. This should be familiar to anybody who has worked with objects in JavaScript, where object-style access via the dot notation can be used in parallel with dictionary-style access via square brackets. As MongoDB uses JavaScript heavily internally, this choice of notation is unsurprising. JSON is JavaScript Object Notation, afterall. The dot notation can also be used in update statements with update modifiers such as $set to set the value of an individual sub-property:

```
# update modifiers such as $set also support the dot notation
dbh.users.update({"facebook.username":"foofacebook"},
    {"$set":{"facebook.username":"bar"}}, safe=True)
```

This use of embedded sub-documents is useful, but perhaps even more useful is to embed multiple sub-documents under a single key. In other words, a property whose value is a list or array of sub-documents. In MongoDB, this is a legal and very useful construct. This is a very natural way to model one-to-many relationships, or parent-child relationships. Consider the example of a "user" document which can reference multiple email addresses for that user. In the relational model, this would typically be achieved with two tables—one for users, and one for the email addresses associated with each user. A join query could then be used to retrieve a user along which each of its email addresses.

In MongoDB, a natural approach to model a one-to-many relationship would be to simply have a property "emails" on the user document, the value of which is an array containing sub-documents, each representing an associated email account. For example:

```
# A user document demonstrating one-to-many relationships using embedding
# Here we map multiple email addresses (along with whether or not the email
# is the user's primary email address) to a single user.
user_doc = {
    "username":"foouser",
    "emails":[
        {
          "email":"foouser1@example.com",
          "primary":True
        },
        {
          "email":"foouser2@example2.com",
          "primary":False
        },
        {
          "email":"foouser3@example3.com",
          "primary":False
        }
    ]
}
```

Not only does this work, but MongoDB has some specific features to help working with this type of embedded structure. Just as you can query for documents by the value of sub-documents directly embedded in the top-level document, documents can also be located by the value of sub-documents embedded in arrays. To do this, simply use the same dot (".") notation, as described earlier in this section. MongoDB transparently searches through arrays for sub-documents.

Returning to our earlier example of a single user with multiple email addresses, consider the following code:

```
# A user document demonstrating one-to-many relationships using embedding
user_doc = {
    "username":"foouser",
    "emails":[
        {
          "email":"foouser1@example.com",
          "primary":True
        },
```

```
        {
          "email":"foouser2@example2.com",
          "primary":False
        },
        {
          "email":"foouser3@example3.com",
          "primary":False
        }
      ]
}
# Insert the user document
dbh.users.insert(user_doc, safe=True)
# Retrieve the just-inserted document via one of its many email addresses
user_doc_result = dbh.users.find_one({"emails.email":"foouser1@example.com"})
# Assert that the original user document and the query result are the same
assert user_doc == user_doc_result
```

In addition to MongoDB understanding lists of sub-documents to enable querying for
embedded values via the dot notation, there are also useful update modifiers. $pull,
$push and their variants are the most helpful, enabling atomic append and removal of
sub-documents to and from embedded lists. Consider the case where a user no longer
wishes a particular email address to be linked to his or her account. The naive way to
remove that email address from their user document would be to first query for their
user document, modify it in your application code so it no longer contains the removed
email address, and then send an update query to the database. Not only is this cumbersome, it also introduces a race condition, as the underlying user document may have
been modified by another process in between your read and write:

```
# Naive method to remove an email address from a user document
# Cumbersome and has a race condition
user_doc = {
    "username":"foouser",
    "emails":[
        {
          "email":"foouser1@example.com",
          "primary":True
        },
        {
          "email":"foouser2@example2.com",
          "primary":False
        },
        {
          "email":"foouser3@example3.com",
          "primary":False
        }
    ]
}
# Insert the user document
dbh.users.insert(user_doc, safe=True)
# Retrieve the just-inserted document via username
user_doc_result = dbh.users.find_one({"username":"foouser"})
# Remove the "foouser2@example2.com" email address sub-document from the embedded list
del user_doc_result["emails"][1]
```

```
# Now write the new emails property to the database
# May cause data to be lost due to the race between read and write
dbh.users.update({"username":"foouser"},{"$set":{"emails":user_doc_result}},
safe=True)
```

The three most common operations on sub-documents embedded in a list property are: Deletion, insertion and modification. Each of these can be performed atomically with the provided update modifiers. First let's demonstrate the use of $pull to remove the sub-document matching "foouser2@example2.com" in a simple and race-free way:

```
# Atomically remove an email address from a user document race-free using the
# $pull update modifier
user_doc = {
    "username":"foouser",
    "emails":[
        {
         "email":"foouser1@example.com",
         "primary":True
        },
        {
         "email":"foouser2@example2.com",
         "primary":False
        },
        {
         "email":"foouser3@example3.com",
         "primary":False
        }
    ]
}
# Insert the user document
dbh.users.insert(user_doc, safe=True)
# Use $pull to atomically remove the "foouser2@example2.com" email sub-document
dbh.users.update({"username":"foouser"},
    {"$pull":{"emails":{"email":"foouser2@example2.com"}}}, safe=True)
```

In this example, $pull is used to match an embedded document with "email":"foouser2@example2.com" in the "emails" field. $pull will remove the entire document from the array in an atomic fashion, meaning there is no opportunity for a race condition. You can also use query modifiers with $pull, for example to remove all sub-documents with a "primary" value that is not equal to True, you could write the following:

```
# Use $pull to atomically remove all email sub-documents with primary not equal to True
dbh.users.update({"username":"foouser"},
    {"$pull":{"emails":{"primary":{"$ne":True}}}}, safe=True)
```

The full range of query modifiers (see table in Chapter 2) are available for use, including $gt, $lt and so on. Additionally, $pull can be used with arrays containing atoms (numbers, strings, dates, ObjectIDs etc). In other words, $pull doesn't work only with embedded documents—if you store a list of primitive types in an array, you can remove elements atomically with $pull too.

The $push update modifier is used to atomically append an element to an array. At the time of writing, $push can only support adding items to the end of the array—there is no update modifier to add an element to the beginning of an array, or to insert it at an arbitrary index. $push is simple to use, because, unlike $pull, it does not take any field match or conditional arguments.

For example, to atomically add a new email address to our user document, we could use the following query:

```
# Use $push to atomically append a new email sub-document to the user document
new_email = {"email":"fooemail4@exmaple4.com", "primary":False}
dbh.users.update({"username":"foouser"},
    {"$push":{"emails":new_email}}, safe=True)
```

The final case is updating an existing sub-document in-place. This can be achieved using what is called the "positional" operator. The positional operator is represented by the dollar sign ("$"). Basically, it is replaced by the server with the index of the item matched by the document spec. For example, suppose we wish to make our user document's "foouser2@example2.com" email address primary. We could issue the following update query to modify it in-place:

```
# Demonstrate usage of the positional operator ($) to modify
# matched sub-documents in-place.
user_doc = {
    "username":"foouser",
    "emails":[
        {
         "email":"foouser1@example.com",
         "primary":True
        },
        {
         "email":"foouser2@example2.com",
         "primary":False
        },
        {
         "email":"foouser3@example3.com",
         "primary":False
        }
    ]
}
# Insert the user document
dbh.users.insert(user_doc, safe=True)
# Now make the "foouser2@example2.com" email address primrary
dbh.users.update({"emails.email":"foouser2@example2.com"},
    {"$set":{"emails.$.primary":True}}, safe=True)
# Now make the "foouser1@example.com" email address not primary
dbh.users.update({"emails.email":"foouser1@example.com"},
    {"$set":{"emails.$.primary":False}}, safe=True)
```

Note that the $ operator cannot be used with upserts (see section on upserts later in this chapter) additionally it only works with the first matched element.

When working with embedding, it is important to be aware of the performance characteristics of documents and sub-documents in MongoDB. First and foremost, when a document is fetched from the database to answer a query, the entire document—including any and all embedded sub-documents—is loaded into memory. This means that there is no extra cost (aside from the additional network and decode/encode CPU overhead incurred by a larger result set) to fetch embedded data. Once the top-level document has been retrieved, its sub-documents are immediately avaialble, too. Contrast this with a relational schema design utilizing joins, where the database may need to read from one or more additional tables to fetch associated data. Depending on the situation, these joins could impact query performance considerably.

Secondly, it is also very important to be aware that there is a size limit on documents in MongoDB. Additionally, the document size limit has been increased over successive major MongoDB releases. In MongoDB 1.4.x and 1.6.x, the maximum document size was 4MB but in 1.8.x it was increased to 16MB. One can expect that this limit may continue to increase—perhaps eventually to be arbitrarily large—but for now, keep in mind that documents have a finite size when modeling your data.

In practice, it is rare to reach even a 4MB document size, unless the design is such that documents continue to grow over time. For example, a scenario where new properties are created on an hourly or daily basis. In such cases, it is wise to ensure there is some application logic to handle purging old/expired embedded sub-documents to prevent the limit being hit.

Another example would be building a document publishing platform which embedded every single document posted by a user as a sub-document inside of the user document. While performance would be excellent since a single query for the user document could retieve all their published documents in a single shot, it is quite likely that some users would eventually publish more than 16MB of content.

Hence there is often a judgement call to be made when designing MongoDB schemas: To embed, or not to embed.

The alternative to embedding is storing the documents in a separate collection and performing a join in your own application code, by querying twice or more. Usually many-to-many relationships are modeled in this way, while one-to-many relationships are embedded.

Fast Lookups: Using Indexes with MongoDB

The role of indexes in MongoDB is very similar to their role in traditional RDBMS such as MySQL, PostgreSQL, etc. MongoDB offers two kinds of indexes out-of-the-box: Btree indexes and geospatial indexes. The btree indexes in MongoDB are much the same as the equivalents in MySQL or PostgreSQL. When in a relational system you would put an index on a column to get fast lookups on that field, you do an analogous thing in MongoDB by placing an index on a particular property in a collection. Just as with an RDBMS, MongoDB indexes can span multiple fields (a.k.a. compound indexes) —useful if you know in advance that you will be querying based on the value of more than a single property. A compound index would be useful for example if you were querying documents by first name and last name. In MongoDB, btree indexes can have a "direction". This direction is only useful in the case of compound indexes, where the index direction should match the sort direction or range query direction for optimal performance. For example, if you are querying a range (say, A through C) on first name and last name and then sorting in ascending order on last name, your compound index direction should also be ascending.

Using a btree index will incur a performance hit on writes, as the database must now update the index in addition to the data. For this reason, it is wise to choose your indexes carefully. Avoid superfluous indexes if at all possible. Indexes also take up valuable storage—not so much of an issue with on-disk space today given the low price-per-terrabyte—but in memory, too. Your database will run fastest when it resides entirely in memory, and indexes can considerably add to its size. It is a classic Computer Science time vs. space tradeoff scenario.

MongoDB btree indexes can also be used to enforce a unique constraint on a particular property in a collection. By default, the _id primary key property has a unique index created in MongoDB. The unique constraint will prevent the protected property from ever having a duplicate value within the collection. This can be useful for values which are expected to be globally unique in the collection—a common example being usernames. Beware of over-reliance on this feature, however, as in the current implementation of sharding, unique indexes are supported only on the _id property—otherwise they are not enforced globally across the cluster.

Btree indexes also transparently support indexing multi-value properties, that is, properties where the value is an array. Each item in the array will be properly stored in the index to enable fast retrieval of the parent document. This can be useful for performant implementations of tagging, where each tag is stored as a string inside a "tags" list property on the document. Lookups for documents matching one or more of those tags (potentially using the $in query operator) will then be looked up in the "tags" index. Furthermore, btree indexes are equally well supported when placed on embedded sub-documents. If, for example, you store email addresses as embedded sub-documents, and you wish to be able to look up by the value of the email address using an index, MongoDB allows this. Hence the following document and query could take advantage of an index:

```
user_doc = {
    "username":"foouser",
    "emails":[
        {
          "email":"foouser1@example.com",
          "primary":True
        },
        {
          "email":"foouser2@example2.com",
```

```
      "primary":False
    },
    {
      "email":"foouser3@example3.com",
      "primary":False
    }
  ]
}

dbh.users.insert(user_doc)
# If we place an index on property "emails.email",
# e.g. dbh.users.create_index("emails.email")
# this find_one query can use a btree index
user = dbh.users.find_one({"emails.email":"foouser2@example2.com"})
```

Btree indexes in MongoDB are also important when performing server-side sorting of results. Without an index on the property you are sorting by, MongoDB will run out of memory when trying to sort anything greater than a relatively small results set (approx. 4Mb at time of writing). If you expect that you will be sorting result sets larger than 4Mb, you should specify an index on the sort key. It is easy to underestimate this and find exceptions are being raised on queries against larger, real-world data which were not anticipated during development.

To create an index with the PyMongo driver, use the `Collection.create_index()` method. This method can create single-key indexes or compound indexes. For a single-key index, only the key needs to be provided. A compound index is slightly more complicated—a list of 2-tuples (key, direction) must be supplied.

For example to create an index on the `username` property of a collection called `users`, you could write the following:

```
# Create index on username property
dbh.users.create_index("username")
```

To create a compound index, for example on the first_name and last_name, with an ascending direction, you could specify:

```
# Create a compound index on first_name and last_name properties
# with ascending index direction
dbh.users.create_index([("first_name", pymongo.ASCENDING), ("last_name",
pymongo.ASCENDING)])
```

Indexes in MongoDB each have names. By default, MongoDB will generate a name, but you may wish to give a custom name—particularly for compound indexes where the generated names are not especially readable by humans. To give a custom name during creation, supply the `name=<str>` parameter to the `create_index()` method:

```
# Create a compound index called "name_idx" on first_name and last_name properties
# with ascending index direction
dbh.users.create_index([
    ("first_name", pymongo.ASCENDING),
    ("last_name", pymongo.ASCENDING)
    ],
    name="name_idx")
```

It should be noted that index creation locks the database by default. For large collections, index creation can be time consuming. To help mitigate the impact of these operations on live, production databases, MongoDB is capable of building indexes in the background, without blocking database access. Building an index in the background may take slightly longer, and will still cause additional load on the system, but the database should otherwise remain available.

To specify that an index should be built in the background, pass the `background=True` parameter to the `create_index()` method:

```
# Create index in the background
# Database remains usable
dbh.users.create_index("username", background=True)
```

As mentioned earlier in this section, MongoDB btree indexes can be used to enforce a uniqueness constraint on a particular property. Unique constraints can be applied to both single-key indexes and compound indexes. To create an index with a unique constraint, simply pass the `unique=True` parameter to the `create_index()` method:

```
# Create index with unique constraint on username property
dbh.users.create_index("username", unique=True)
```

Be aware that unique indexes in MongoDB do not function exactly the same as indexes in RDBMS systems. In particular, a document with a missing property will be added to the index as if it the value of that property were null. This means that when a unique constraint is added to a btree index in MongoDB, the database will prevent you from having multiple documents in the collection which are missing the indexed property. For example, if you have created a unique index for the `username` property in a users collection, only one document in that collection may be permitted to lack a `username` property. Writes of additional documents without a `username` property will raise an exception. If you try to add a unique index to a collection which already contains duplicates on the specified property, MongoDB will (unsurprisingly) raise an exception. However, if you don't mind throwing away duplicate data, you can instruct MongoDB to drop all but the first document it finds using the `dropDups` or `drop_dups` parameter:

```
# Create index with unique constraint on username property
# instructing MongoDB to drop all duplicates after the first document it finds.
dbh.users.create_index("username", unique=True, drop_dups=True)
# Could equally be written:
# dbh.users.create_index("username", unique=True, dropDups=True)
```

Over time, your schema may evolve and you may find that a particular index is no longer needed. Fortunately, indexes are easy to remove in MongoDB. The `Collection.drop_index()` method deletes one index at a time. If you created your index with a custom name (as described above), you must supply this same name to the `drop_index()` method in order to delete it. For example:

```
# Create index on username property called "username_idx"
dbh.users.create_index("username", name="username_idx")
# Delete index called "username_idx"
dbh.users.drop_index("username_idx")
```

If, on the other hand, you did not give your index a custom name, you can delete by passing the original index specifier. For example:

```
# Create a compound index on first_name and last_name properties
# with ascending index direction
dbh.users.create_index([("first_name", pymongo.ASCENDING), ("last_name",
pymongo.ASCENDING)])
# Delete this index
dbh.users.drop_index([("first_name", pymongo.ASCENDING), ("last_name",
pymongo.ASCENDING)])
```

All indexes in a collection can be dropped in a single statement using the `Collection.drop_indexes()` method.

If you wish to programatically inspect the indexes on your collections from Python, you can use the `Collection.index_information()` method. This returns a dictionary in which each key is the name of an index. The value associated with each key is an additional dictionary. These second-level dictionaries always contain a special key called key, which is an entry containing the original index specifier—including index direction. This original index specifier was the data passed to the `create_index()` method when the index was first created. The second-level dictionaries may also contain additional options such as unique constraints and so on.

Location-based Apps with MongoDB: GeoSpatial Indexing

As mentioned in the previous section on indexes, MongoDB has support for two kinds of index: Btree and geospatial. Btree indexes have been covered quite thoroughly in the preceeding section, however we have not yet described GeoSpatial indexes.

First of all, let us discuss why geospatial indexing might be useful at all. Many apps today are being built with the requirement of location-awareness. Typically this translates into features where points of interest (POI) near a particular user location may be rapidly retrieved from a database. For example, a location-aware mobile app might wish to quickly fetch a list of nearby coffeeshops, based upon the current GPS coordinates. The complicating issue, fundamentally, is that the world is both quite large and quite full of interesting points—and so to try to answer such a query by iterating through the entire list of all POIs in the world to find ones which are nearby would take an unacceptably long time. Hence the need for some sort of GeoSpatial indexing, to speed up these searches.

Fortunately for anybody tasked with building location-aware applications, MongoDB is one of the rare few databases with out-of-the-box support for geospatial indexing. MongoDB uses geohashing, a public domain algorithm developed by Gustavo Niemeyer, which translates geographic proximity into lexical proximity. Hence, a database supporting range queries (such as MongoDB) can be efficiently used to query for points near and within bounds.

It should be noted that at present, MongoDB's geospatial indexing support is limited purely to point-based querying. The supplied operators can only be used for finding individual points—not routes or sub-shapes.

MongoDB provides the $near and $within operators which constitute the primary means for performing geospatial queries in the system. Using $near, you can efficiently sort documents in a collection by their proximity to a given point. The $within operator allows you to specify a bounds for the query. Supported boundary definitions include $box for a rectangular shape, $circle for a circle. In MongoDB 1.9 and up, the $poly gon operator allows for convex and concave polygon boundaries.

Before you can use the geospatial queries, you must have a geospatial index. In MongoDB versions up to and including 1.8.x, geospatial indexes are limited to a single index per collection. This means that each document can have only one location property queried efficiently by MongoDB. This can have some important implications for schema design which is why it is good to know from the outset.

 Geospatial indexes by default limit acceptable values for the location property on documents to those within GPS. That is, co-ordinates must be in the range -180 .. +180. If you have co-ordinates outside of this range, MongoDB will raise an exception when you attempt to create the geospatial index on the colleciton. If you wish to index values outside of the range of regular GPS, you can specify this at index creation time.

The location property on your documents must be either an array or sub-document where the first two items are the x and y co-ordinates to be indexed. The order of the co-ordinates (whether x,y or y,x) does not matter so long as it is consistent on all documents. For example, your document could look like any of the following:

```
# location property is an array with x,y ordering
user_doc = {
    "username":"foouser",
    "user_location":[x,y]
}

# location property is an array with y,x ordering
user_doc = {
    "username":"foouser",
    "user_location":[y,x]
}

import bson
# location property is a sub-document with y,x ordering
loc = bson.SON()
loc["y"] = y
loc["x"] = x
user_doc = {
    "username":"foouser",
    "user_location":loc
}
```

```
import bson
# location property is a sub-document with x,y ordering
loc = bson.SON()
loc["x"] = x
loc["y"] = y
user_doc = {
    "username":"foouser",
    "user_location":loc
}
```

 Note that in Python the default dictionary type (dict class), order is not preserved. When using location in a sub-document from Python, use a bson.SON object instead. bson.SON comes with the PyMongo driver, and is used in exactly the same way as Python's dict class.

Once the documents in your collection have their location properties correctly formed, we can create the geospatial index. As with btree indexes, geospatial indexes in MongoDB are created with PyMongo's Collection.create_index() method. Due to the one-geospatial-index-per-collection limitation in MongoDB versions up to and including 1.8.x, if you are planning to query by other properties in addition to the location property, you can make your geospatial index a compound index. For exmaple, if you know that you will be searching your collection by both "username" and "user_location" properties, you could create a compound geo index across both fields. This can help to work around the single geospatial index limitation in many cases.

Returning to our example of documents in a collection called "users" with the location property being "user_location", we would create a geospatial index with the following statement:

```
# Create geospatial index on "user_location" property.
dbh.users.create_index([("user_location", pymongo.GEO2D)])
```

To create a compound geospatial index which would let us query efficiently on location and username, we could issue this statement:

```
# Create geospatial index on "user_location" property.
dbh.users.create_index([("user_location", pymongo.GEO2D), ("username",
pymongo.ASCENDING)])
```

Now that we have geospatial indexes available, we can try out some efficient location-based queries. The $near operator is pretty easy to understand, so we shall start there. As has already been explained, $near will sort query results by proximity to specified point. By default, $near will try to find the closest 100 results.

An important performance consideration which is not mentioned clearly in the official MongoDB documentation is that when using $near, you will almost always want to specify a maximum distance on the query. Without a clamp on the maximum distance, in order to return the specified number of results (default 100) MongoDB has to search through the entire database. This takes a lot of time. In most cases, a max distance of around 5 degrees should be sufficient. Since we are using decimal degrees (a.k.a GPS) co-ordinates, the units of max distance is degrees. 1 degree is roughly 69 miles. If you only care about a relatively small set of results (for example, the nearest 10 coffee shops), limiting the query to 10 results should also aid performance.

Let's start with an example of finding the nearest 10 users to the point 40, 40 limiting to a max distance of 5 degrees:

```
# Find the 10 users nearest to the point 40, 40 with max distance 5 degrees
nearest_users = dbh.users.find(
    {"user_location":
        {"$near" : [40, 40],
         "$maxDistance":5}}).limit(10)
# Print the users
for user in nearest_users:
    # assume user_location property is array x,y
    print "User %s is at location %s,%s" %(user["username"], user["user_location"][0],
        user["user_location"][1])
```

Next let us try using the $within geospatial operator to find points within a certain boundary. This can be useful when searching for POI's in a specific county/city or even well-defined neighbourhood within a city. In the real world, these boundaries are fuzzy and changing constantly, however there are good enough databases available for them to be useful.

To specify a rectangle to search within, you simply provide the lower-left and top-right co-ordinates as elements in an array. For example:

```
box = [[50.73083, -83.99756], [50.741404,  -83.988135]]
```

We could query for points within this bound by using the following geospatial query:

```
box = [[50.73083, -83.99756], [50.741404,  -83.988135]]
users_in_boundary = dbh.users.find({"user_location":{"$within": {"$box":box}}})
```

To specify a citcle to search within, you just supply the center point and the radius. As with $maxDistance mentioned previously, the units of the radius are degrees. Here is how we could make a geospatial lookup for 10 users within a radius of 5 degress centered at the point 40, 40:

```
users_in_circle = dbh.users.find({"user_location":{"$within":{"$center":[40, 40,
5]}}}).limit(10)
```

Notice that with the circle boundary using $center, we pass an array, the first two values of which are the co-ordinates of the center and the third parameter is the radius (in degrees).

All the queries we've mentioned so far which make use of a geospatial index actually are not entirely accurate. This is because they use a flat earth model where each arc degree of latitude and longitude translates to the same distance everywhere on the earth. In reality, the earth is a sphere and so these values differ depending upon where you are. Fortunately, MongoDB in 1.8.x and up implements a spherical model of the earth for geospatial queries.

The new spherical model can be used by employing the $nearSphere and $circle Sphere variants on the $near and $circle operators. MongoDB's spherical model has a few extra caveats. First and foremost, you must use (longitude, latitude) ordering of your co-ordinates. While there are many other application and formats which use the (latitude, longitude) ordering, you should be careful to re-order to use with MongoDB's spherical model. Secondly, unlike the $near and $center operators we just described, the units for distances with $nearSphere and $centerSphere are always expressed in radians. This includes when using $maxDistance with $nearSphere or $centerSphere. Luckily, it is not difficult to convert from a more humanly-understandable unit such as kilometers to radians. To translate from kilometers to radians, simply divide the kilometer value by the radius of the earth which is approximately 6371 km (or 3959 miles). To demonstrate, let's try our earlier example of finding the 10 users nearest to the point 40,40 with a max distance of 5 km—but this time using the spherical model:

```
# Find the 10 users nearest to the point 40, 40 with max distance 5 degrees
# Uses the spherical model provided by MongoDB 1.8.x and up

earth_radius_km = 6371.0
max_distance_km = 5.0
max_distance_radians = max_distance_km / earth_radius_km
nearest_users = dbh.users.find(
    {"user_location":
        {"$nearSphere" : [40, 40],
         "$maxDistance":max_distance_radians}}).limit(10)
# Print the users
for user in nearest_users:
    # assume user_location property is array x,y
    print "User %s is at location %s,%s" %(user["username"], user["user_location"][0],
        user["user_location"][1])
```

Code Defensively to Avoid KeyErrors and Other Bugs

One of the tradeoffs of a document-oriented database versus a relational database is that the database does not enforce schema for you. For this reason, when working with MongoDB you must be vigilant in your handling of database results. Do not blindly assume that results will always have the properties you expect.

Check for their presence before accessing them. Although Python will generally raise a KeyError and stop execution, depending on your application this still may result in loss of data integrity. Consider the case of updating every document in a collection one-by-one—a single unforeseen KeyError could leave the database in an inconsistent state, with some documents having been updated and others not.

For example,

```
all_user_emails = []
for username in ("jill", "sam", "cathy"):
    user_doc = dbh.users.find_one({"username":username})
    # KeyError will be raised if any of these does not exist
    dbh.emails.insert({"email":user_doc["email"]})
```

Sometimes you will want to have a default fallback to avoid KeyErrors should a document be returned which is missing a property required by your program. The Python dict class' get method easily lets you specify a default value for a property should it be missing.

Often it makes sense to use this defensively. For example, imagine we have a collection of user documents. Some users have a "score" property set to a number, while others do not. It would be safe to have a default fallback of zero (0) in the case that no score property is present. We can take a missing score to mean a zero score. The dict class's get method lets us do this easily:

```
total_score = 0
for username in ("jill", "sam", "cathy"):
    user_doc = dbh.users.find_one({"username":username})
    total_score += user_doc.get("score", 0)
```

This approach can also work well when looping over embedded lists. For example, to defensively handle the case where a document representing a particular product does not yet have a list of suppliers embedded (perhaps because it is not yet on the market, or is no longer being produced) you might write code like this:

```
# Email each supplier of this product.
# Default value is the empty list so no special casing
# is needed if the suppliers property is not present.
for supplier in product_doc.get("suppliers", []):
    email_supplier(supplier)
```

MongoDB also makes no guarantees about the type of a property's value on a given document.

In most RDBMS implementations (the notable exception I'm aware of being SQLite) the database will quite rigorously enforce column types. If you try to insert a string into an integer column, the database will reject the write.

MongoDB, on the other hand, will only in exceptional circumstances reject such writes. If you set the value of a property on one document to be a string and on another document in the same collection set the value of that property to a number, it will very happily store that.

```
# Perfectly legal insert - MongoDB will not complain
dbh.users.insert({"username":"janedoe"})
# Also perfectly legal - MongoDB will not complain
dbh.users.insert({"username":1337})
```

When you couple this with Python's willingness to let you forgo explicitly typing your variables, you can soon run into trouble. Perhaps the most common scenario is when writing inputs from Web applications to the database. Most WSGI-based Python frameworks will send you all HTTP POST and GET parameter values as strings—regardless of whether or not they are in fact strings.

Thus it is easy to insert or update a numeric property with a value that is a string. The best way, of course, to avoid errors of this nature is to prevent the wrong type of data ever being written to the database in the first place. Thus, in the context of a Web application, validating and/or coercing the types of any inputs to write queries before issuing them is strongly advised. You may consider using the FormEncode or Colander Python libraries to help with such validation.

Update-or-Insert: Upserts in MongoDB

A relatively common task in a database-powered application is to update an existing entry, or if not found insert it as a new record. MongoDB conveniently supports this as a single operation, freeing you from having to implement your own "if-exists-update-else-insert" logic. 10gen refer to this type of write operation as an "upsert".

In PyMongo, there are three possible methods one can use to perform an upsert. These are `Collection.save()`, `Collection.update()` and `Collection.find_and_modify()`. We shall start by describing `Collection.save()` as it is the most straight forward method.

In the earlier section "Inserting a Document into a Collection" we used the `Collection.insert()` method to write a new document to the collection. However, we could have just as easily used the `save()` method. `save()` offers almost identical functionality to `insert()` with the following exceptions: `save()` can perform upserts and `save()` cannot insert multiple documents in a single call.

`save()` is quite easy to understand. If you pass it a document without an `_id` property it will perform an `insert()`, creating a brand new document. If, on the other hand, you pass it a document which contains an `_id` property it will update the existing document corresponding to that `_id` value, overwriting the already-present document with the document passed to `save()`.

This is the essence of an upsert: If a document already exists, update it. Otherwise create a new document.

`save()` can be useful because it supports both writing new documents and modifying existing documents, most likely ones retrieved from MongoDB via a read query. Having a single method which is capable of both modes of operation reduces the need for conditional handling in your client code, thus simplifying your program.

More useful, perhaps, is the "upsert=True" parameter which may be passed to `Collection.update()`. As has been discussed in the section "Updating Documents in a Collection" and is further described in the section "MongoDB Update Modifiers", the `update()` method supports the use of "update modifiers". These rich operators enable you to perform writes more complex than the basic "overwrite but keep existing _id" semantics of the `save()` method.

For example, imagine you are writing a method, `edit_or_add_session()`. This method either edits an existing document, or inserts a new one. Furthermore, semantics of the method dictate that the method will always be called with a session_id, but that the session_id may or may not already be present in the database. The naive implementation would first query to see whether a session document already existed, then conditionally either insert a new session document or update the existing document:

```
# Naive, bad implementation without upsert=True
def edit_or_add_session(description, session_id):
    # We must query first, becase we don't know whether this session_id already exists.
    # If we attempt to update a non-existent document, no write will occur.
    session_doc = dbh.sessions.find_one({"session_id":session_id})
    if session_doc:
        dbh.sessions.update({"session_id":session_id},
            {"$set":{"session_description":description}}, safe=True)
    else:
        dbh.sessions.insert({"session_description":description,
"session_id":session_id},
            safe=True)
```

However, by employing the upsert feature of `Collection.update()`, this can be implemented in a single method call—simplifying the code considerably and eliminating the need for an extra read query:

```
# Good implementation using upsert=True
def edit_or_add_session(description, session_id):
    dbh.sessions.update({"session_id":session_id},
        {"$set":{"session_description":description}}, safe=True, upsert=True)
```

Note that we could not have implemented the above semantics using `Cursor.save()` because we are testing for existence on the property "session_id" rather than "_id". Recall that the `save()` upsert method only works with "_id".

The trick to understanding upserts with the `update()` method is to consider the two execution cases seperately. In the case that the document already exists, then the update document will be processed normally—just as with a regular `update()` call without the "upsert=True" parameter. However, in the case that the document does not already exist, the document written (upserted) will match both the document spec supplied as the first argument to the `update()` call and the update document with any modifiers it contains. In other words, the observed behaviour is that the document is first created with the properties specified in the document spec—in this case, `"session_id":ses sion_id`—and then the update document is executed against that. That may not accurately reflect what is happening internally in the daemon or driver, but that is equivalent to whatever does go on.

Atomic Read-Write-Modify: MongoDB's findAndModify

We've already introduced the atomic update modifiers supported by MongoDB. These are very powerful and enable race-free write operations of many kinds—including array manipulation and increment/decrement. However, it is often necessary to be able to modify the document atomically, and also return the result of the atomic operation—in a single step.

For example, imagine a billing system. Each user document has an "account_balance" property. There may be writes which alter the account balance—let's say an account top-up event which adds money to the account, and a purchase action which takes money from the account. Consider the following implementation:

```
# User X adds $20 to his/her account, so we atomically increment
# account_balance
dbh.users.update({"username":username}, {"$inc":{"account_balance":20}}, safe=True)
# Fetch the updated account balance to display to user
new_account_balance = dbh.users.find_one({"username":username},
    {"account_balance":1})["account_balance"]
```

This will work fine assuming no other writes to the account balance occur between the write and read operations. There is an obvious race condition. If a purchase action were to take place between the balance update and the balance read, the user may be displeased to be presented with a post-payment balance of less than what they expected!

```
# User X adds $20 to his/her account, so we atomically increment
# account_balance
dbh.users.update({"username":username}, {"$inc":{"account_balance":20}}, safe=True)

# In the meantime, in another thread or process, there is a payment operation,
# which decrements the account balance:
dbh.users.update({"username":username}, {"$dec":{"account_balance":5}}, safe=True)

# Fetch the updated account balance to display to user
new_account_balance = dbh.users.find_one({"username":username},
    {"account_balance":1})["account_balance"]
```

What you want in this kind of situation is a way to update the account balance and return the new value in a single, atomic operation. MongoDB's findAndModify command allows you to do just this. PyMongo provides a wrapper around findAndModify in the Collection.find_and_modify() method. Using this method, we can rewrite the code to a single, atomic operation:

```
# User X adds $20 to his/her account, so we atomically increment
# account_balance and return the resulting document
ret = dbh.users.find_and_modify({"username":username},
    {"$inc":{"account_balance":20}}, safe=True, new=True)
new_account_balance = ret["account_balance"]
```

Fast Accounting Pattern

Many of the applications people are building today are realtime with very large data sets. That is to say, users expect changes they make to be reflected within the application instantly. For example if a user wins a new high score in a multiplayer game, they expect the high score table in the game to be updated immediately. However, it may not be a single high score table which must be updated. Perhaps you are also ranking by high score this week, or this month, or even this year. Furthermore, as the application developer you may wish to keep a detailed log of each change—including when it occured, what the client IP address was, the software version of the client, etc.—per user for analytics purposes.

This pattern isn't limited to high scores. Similar high performance accounting requirements exist for in-app social activity feeds, billing systems which charge per byte, and so on. Not only do these counts need to be fast to read from the database, they needs to be quick to write. Additionally, with potentially millions of users, the data set can grow very large, very quickly.

You might be tempted to keep only a detailed log, with one document per change. Totals for the various time periods can then be calculated by an aggregate query across the collection. This may work well initially, with only hundreds or thousands of documents to be aggregated to compute the result. However when the number of these documents grows into the millions or even billions—which they may easily do in a successful application—this approach will quickly become intractable.

Of course, as with many problems in Computer Science, the solution is ultimately a form of caching. MongoDB and its document-oriented data model gives us a nice idiom for this kind of period-based accounting, however. Given that we are counting on a per-user basis, we can utilize embedded sub-documents containing property names derived from time period. Consider for example a high score table supporting resolutions of week, month and total (across all time).

For the weekly resolution score counts, we can name the properties after the current week number. To disambiguate over multiple years, we can include the four-digit year in the key:

```
# Store weekly scores in sub-document
user_doc = {
    "scores_weekly":{
        "2011-01":10,
        "2011-02":3,
        "2011-06":20
    }
}
```

To fetch the score for this week, we simply execute the following simple dictionary lookup:

```
# Fetch the score for the current week
import datetime
now = datetime.datetime.utcnow()
current_year = now.year
current_week = now.isocalendar()[1]
# Default missing keys to a score of zero
user_doc["scores_weekly"].get("%d-%d" %(current_year, current_week), 0)
```

Such a lookup is incredibly fast. There is no aggregation to perform whatsoever. With this pattern, we can also write very quickly and safely. Because we are counting, we can take advantage of MongoDB's atomic increment and decrement update modifiers, $inc and $dec. Atomic update operators are great because they ensure the underlying data is in a consistent state and help to avoid nasty race conditions. Especially when dealing with billing, accurate counts are very important.

Imagine we wish to increment the user's score for this week by 24. We can do so with the following query:

```
# Update the score for the current week
import datetime
username = "foouser"
now = datetime.datetime.utcnow()
current_year = now.year
current_week = now.isocalendar()[1]
# Use atomic update modifier to increment by 24
dbh.users.update({"username":username},
    {"$inc":{"scores_weekly.%s-%s" %(current_year, current_week):24}},
    safe=True)
```

If the application needs to track multiple time-periods, these can be represented as additional sub-documents:

```
# Store daily, weekly, monthly and total scores in user document
user_doc = {
    "scores_weekly":{
        "2011-01":10,
        "2011-02":3,
        "2011-06":20
    },
    "scores_daily":{
        "2011-35":2,
        "2011-59":7,
        "2011-83":15
    },
    "scores_monthly":{
        "2011-09":30,
        "2011-10":43,
        "2011-11":24
    },
    "score_total":123
}
```

Of course, in your writes, you should increment the counts for each time period:

```
# Update the score for the current week
import datetime
username = "foouser"
now = datetime.datetime.utcnow()
current_year = now.year
current_month = new.month
current_week = now.isocalendar()[1]
current_day = now.timetuple().tm_yday
# Use atomic update modifier to increment by 24
dbh.users.update({"username":username},
    {"$inc":{
        "scores_weekly.%s-%s" %(current_year, current_week):24,
        "scores_daily.%s-%s" %(current_year, current_day):24,
        "scores_monthly.%s-%s" %(current_year, current_month):24,
```

```
        "score_total":24,
        }
    },
    safe=True)
```

In cases where you want to report the count immediately after the update, that can be achieved by using the findAndModify command (described in previous section) to return the new document after the update has been applied.

This pattern can help greatly with high speed counting. If more detailed logs are still needed—such as when each action took place—feel free to maintain those in a separate collection. This summary data is most useful for extremely fast reads and writes.

## CHAPTER 4

MongoDB with Web Frameworks

While MongoDB can be used in all sorts of applications, its most obvious role is as the database backend for a web application. These days, a great many mobile and tablet applications are functioning as "fat clients" to the same HTTP-based API's as browser-based web applications; hence mobile and tablet apps need the same sort of backend database infrastructure as more traditional web apps.

Many organizations and engineers are finding the advantages of MongoDB's document-oriented architecture compelling enough to migrate parts or even entire applications from traditional RDBMS such as MySQL to MongoDB. Numerous well-known companies have built their whole application from the ground up on MongoDB.

It is my opinion that for the vast majority of web, mobile and tablet applications, MongoDB is a better starting point than RDBMS technology such as MySQL. This chapter is an attempt to get you off the ground using MongoDB with three common Python web frameworks: Pylons, Pyramid and Django.

Pylons 1.x and MongoDB

Pylons is one of the older WSGI-based Python web frameworks, dating back to September 2005. Pylons reached version 1.0 in 2010 and is considered very stable at this point. In fact, not much development is planned for Pylons 1.x any more; all new development is happening in Pyramid (see "Pyramid and MongoDB" on page 49 for details). The Pylons philosophy is the precise opposite of "one-size-fits-all." Application developers are free to choose from the various database, templating, session store options available. This kind of framework is excellent when you aren't exactly sure what pieces you will need when you are starting work on your application. If it turns out you need to use an XML-based templating system, you are free to do so.

The existence of Pyramid aside, Pylons 1.x is a very capable and stable framework. As Pylons is so modular, it is easy to add MongoDB support to it.

First you need to create a virtual environment for your project. These instructions assume you have the `virtualenv` tool installed on your system. Install instructions for the `virtualenv` tool are provided in the first chapter of this book.

To create the virtual environment and install Pylons along with its dependencies, run the following commands:

```
virtualenv --no-site-packages myenv
cd myenv
source bin/activate
easy_install pylons
```

Now we have Pylons installed in a virtual environment. Create another directory named whatever you like in which to create your Pylons 1.x project, change your working directory to it, then execute:

```
paster create -t pylons
```

You will be prompted to enter a name for your project, along with which template engine you want to use and whether or not you want the SQLAlchemy Object-Relational Mapper (ORM). The defaults ("mako" for templating engine, False to SQLAlchemy) are fine for our purposes—not least since we are demonstrating a NoSQL database!

After I ran the `paster create` command, a "pylonsfoo" directory (I chose "pylonsfoo" as my project name) was created with the following contents:

```
MANIFEST.in
README.txt
development.ini
docs
ez_setup.py
pylonsfoo
pylonsfoo.egg-info
setup.cfg
setup.py
test.ini
```

Next you need to add the PyMongo driver as a dependency for your project. Change your working directory to the just-created directory named after your project. Open the `setup.py` file present in it with your favourite editor. Change the `install_requires` list to include the string `pymongo`. Your file should look something like this:

```
try:
    from setuptools import setup, find_packages
except ImportError:
    from ez_setup import use_setuptools
    use_setuptools()
    from setuptools import setup, find_packages

setup(
    name='pylonsfoo',
    version='0.1',
```

```
        description='',
        author='',
        author_email='',
        url='',
        install_requires=[
            "Pylons>=1.0", "pymongo",
        ],
        setup_requires=["PasteScript>=1.6.3"],
        packages=find_packages(exclude=['ez_setup']),
        include_package_data=True,
        test_suite='nose.collector',
        package_data={'pylonsfoo': ['i18n/*/LC_MESSAGES/*.mo']},
        #message_extractors={'pylonsfoo': [
        #        ('**.py', 'python', None),
        #        ('templates/**.mako', 'mako', {'input_encoding': 'utf-8'}),
        #        ('public/**', 'ignore', None)]},
        zip_safe=False,
        paster_plugins=['PasteScript', 'Pylons'],
        entry_points="""
    [paste.app_factory]
    main = pylonsfoo.config.middleware:make_app

    [paste.app_install]
    main = pylons.util:PylonsInstaller
    """,
)
```

Now you need to fetch the PyMongo driver into your virtual environment. It is easy to do this by executing:

```
python setup.py develop
```

Your Pylons app is now ready to be configured with a MongoDB connection. First, we shall create a config file for development

```
cp development.ini.sample development.ini
```

Next open the file development.ini in your favourite editor. Underneath the section [app:main] add the following two variables, changing the URI and database names to whatever works for your set up:

```
mongodb.url = mongodb://localhost
mongodb.db_name = mydb
```

You can now try starting your project with the following command:

```
paster serve --reload development.ini
```

You should see the following output:

```
Starting subprocess with file monitor
Starting server in PID 82946.
serving on http://127.0.0.1:5000
```

If you open the URL *http://localhost:5000/* in a web browser, you should see the default Pylons page. This means that you have correctly set up your project. However, we do not yet have a way to talk to MongoDB.

Now that the configuration is in place, we can tell Pylons how to connect to MongoDB and where to make the PyMongo connection available to our application. Pylons provides a convenient place for this in <project_name>/lib/app_globals.py. Edit this file and change the contents to the following:

```
from beaker.cache import CacheManager
from beaker.util import parse_cache_config_options
from pymongo import Connection
from pylons import config

class Globals(object):
    """Globals acts as a container for objects available throughout the
    life of the application

    """

    def __init__(self, config):
        """One instance of Globals is created during application
        initialization and is available during requests via the
        'app_globals' variable

        """
        mongodb_conn = Connection(config['mongodb.url'])
        self.mongodb = mongodb_conn[config['mongodb.db_name']]
        self.cache = CacheManager(**parse_cache_config_options(config))
```

Once this has been set up, a PyMongo Database instance will be available to your Pylons controller actions through the globals object. To demonstrate, we will create a new controller named "mongodb" with the following command:

```
paster controller mongodb
```

You should see a file named mongodb.py in the <project_name>/controllers directory. For demonstration purposes, we shall modify it to increment a counter document in MongoDB every time the controller action is run.

Open this file with your editor. Modify it to look like the following (remembering to change the from pylonsfoo import line into whatever you named your project):

```
import logging

from pylons import app_globals as g, request, response, session, tmpl_context as c, url
from pylons.controllers.util import abort, redirect

from pylonsfoo.lib.base import BaseController, render

log = logging.getLogger(__name__)

class MongodbController(BaseController):

    def index(self):
        new_doc = g.mongodb.counters.find_and_modify({"counter_name":"test_counter"},
            {"$inc":{"counter_value":1}}, new=True, upsert=True , safe=True)
        return "MongoDB Counter Value: %s" % new_doc["counter_value"]
```

Once you have saved these changes, in a web browser open the URL *http://localhost:5000/mongodb/index*. Each time you load this page, you should see a document in the counters collection be updated with its `counter_value` property incremented by 1.

Pyramid and MongoDB

Pyramid is an unopinionated web framework which resulted from the merge of the `repoz.bfg` framework into the Pylons umbrella project (not to be confused with Pylons 1.x, the web framework). Pyramid can be considered to be a bit like a Pylons 2.0; it is a clean break, a completely new codebase with no code-level backwards compatibility with Pylons 1.x.

However, many of the concepts are very similar to the older Pylons 1.x. Pyramid is where all the new development is happening, and it has fantastic code test coverage and documentation. This section is only intended to be a brief introduction to setting up a Pyramid project with a MongoDB connection. To learn more, refer to the excellent Pyramid book and other resources available free online at *http://docs.pylonsproject.org/*.

On its own, Pyramid is just a framework, a set of libraries you can use. Projects are most easily started from a what is known as a scaffold. A scaffold is like a project skeleton which sets up plumbing and placeholders for your code.

A number of different scaffolds are included with Pyramid, offering different persistence options, URL mappers and session implementations. Conveniently enough, there is a scaffold called `pyramid_mongodb` which will build out a skeleton project with MongoDB support for you. `pyramid_mongodb` eliminates the need for you to worry about writing the glue code to make a MongoDB connection available for request processing in Pyramid.

As with Pylons 1.x, to start using Pyramid you first need to create a virtual environment for your project. These instructions assume you have the `virtualenv` tool installed on your system. Install instructions for the `virtualenv` tool are provided in the first chapter of this book.

To create the virtual environment and install Pyramid and its dependencies, run the following commands:

```
virtualenv --no-site-packages myenv
cd myenv
source bin/activate
easy_install pyramid
```

Take note of the line sourcing the `bin/activate` script. It is important to remember to do this once in every shell to make the virtual environment active. Without this step, your default system Python install will be invoked, which does not have Pyramid installed.

Now your virtual environment has Pyramid and all its dependencies installed. How-ever, you still need pyramid_mongodb and its dependencies like PyMongo etc. Run the following command to install pyramid_mongodb in your virtual environment:

```
easy_install pyramid_mongodb
```

With Pyamid and pyramid_mongodb installed in your virtual environment, you are ready to create a Pyramid project with MongoDB support. Decide upon a project directory and a project name. From that project directory execute in the shell:

```
paster create -t pyramid_mongodb <project_name>
```

After I ran the paster create command, a "mongofoo" directory (I chose "mongofoo" as my project name) was created with the following contents:

```
README.txt
development.ini
mongofoo
mongofoo.egg-info
production.ini
setup.cfg
setup.py
```

The default configuration files tell Pyramid to connect to a MongoDB server on local host, and a database called "mydb". If you need to change that, simply edit the mon godb.url and mongodb.db_name settings in the INI-files. Note that if you do not have a MongoDB server running at the address configured in the INI-file, your Pyramid project will fail to start.

Before you can run or test your app, you need to execute:

```
python setup.py develop
```

This will ensure any additional dependencies are installed. To run your project in debug mode, simply execute:

```
paster serve --reload development.ini
```

If all went well, you should see output like the following:

```
Starting subprocess with file monitor
Starting server in PID 54019.
serving on 0.0.0.0:6543 view at http://127.0.0.1:6543
```

You can now open *http://localhost:6543/* in a web browser and see your Pyramid project, with the default template. If you made it this far, Pyramid is correctly installed and pyramid_mongodb was able to successfully connect to the configured MongoDB server.

The pyramid_mongodb scaffold sets up your Pyramid project in such a way that there is a PyMongo Database object attached to each request object. To demonstrate how to use this, open the file <project_name>/views.py in your favourite editor. There should be a skeletal Python function named my_view:

```
def my_view(request):
    return {'project':'mongofoo'}
```

This is a very simple Pyramid view callable. Pyramid view callables are similar to controller actions in Pylons 1.x, and are where much of the application-defined request processing occurs. Since view callables are passed an instance of a request object, which in turn has a property containing the PyMongo Database object, this is an ideal place to interact with MongoDB.

Imagine a somewhat contrived example whereby we wish to insert a document into a collection called "page_hits" each time the my_view view callable is executed. We could do the following:

```
import datetime
def my_view(request):
    new_page_hit = {"timestamp":datetime.datetime.utcnow(), "url":request.url}
    request.db.page_hits.insert(new_page_hit, safe=True)
    return {"project":"mongofoo"}
```

If you now reload the web page at *http://localhost:6543* you should see a collection called "page_hits" in the MongoDB database you configured in your INI-file. In this collection there should be a single document for each time the view has been called.

From here, you should be well on your way to building web applications with Pyramid and MongoDB.

Django and MongoDB

Django is proabably the most widely-used Python web framework. It has an excellent community and many plugins and extension modules. The Django philosophy is the opposite of Pylons or Pyramid; it offers one well-integrated package including its own database and ORM layer, templating system, URL mapper, admin interface and so on.

There are a number of options for running Django with MongoDB. Since the Django ORM is such an integral part of Django, there is a project known as Django MongoDB Engine which attempts to provide a MongoDB backend for the Django ORM. However, this approach heavily abstracts the underlying query language and data model, along with many of the low-level details discussed in the course of the book. If you are already familiar with the Django ORM, enjoy using it, and are willing to use a fork of Django, Django MongoDB Engine is worth a look. You can find more information at the website *http://django-mongodb.org/*.

Our recommended approach for now is to use the PyMongo driver directly with Django. Be aware, however, that with this method, the Django components which depend on the Django ORM (admin interface, session store etc) will not work with MongoDB. There is another project called Mango which attempts to provide MongoDB-backed session and authentication support for Django. You can find Mango at *https://github.com/vpulim/mango*.

10gen have made a sample Django app with PyMongo integration available. This sample app can be found at *https://github.com/mdirolf/DjanMon*. We shall step through running the sample Django + MongoDB app on your local machine, and examine how it sets up the MongoDB connection.

First, download the sample Django project. If you already have the git command line tools installed, you can run git `clone` *https://github.com/mdirolf/DjanMon.git*. Otherwise, simply click the "Download" button at *https://github.com/mdirolf/DjanMon*.

In order to successfully run the sample app, you will need to build a Python virtual environment with Django, pymongo and PIL installed. As with Pylons and Pyramid, you will first need to have the `virtualenv` tool installed on your system—details on how to do this are covered in the first chapter of this book. Once you have `virtualenv` installed, chose a directory in which to store virtual env, then execute the following shell commands in it:

```
virtualenv --no-site-packages djangoenv
cd djangoenv
source bin/activate
pip install django pymongo PIL
```

This will create your virtual environment, activate it and then install Django, the PyMongo driver and the PIL image manipulation library (required by the demo app) into it. Assuming this all succeeded, you are ready to start the sample app development server. Note that the sample app expects a MongoDB server to be running on `localhost`.

Now we can run 10gen's Django demonstration app. Change your current working directory to your copy of the "DjanMon" project. There should be a file called `man age.py` in the current working directory. The app can be run with the Django development server with the command:

```
python manage.py runserver
```

You should see output on the console like the following:

```
Validating models...

0 errors found
Django version 1.3, using settings 'DjanMon.settings'
Development server is running at http://127.0.0.1:8000/
Quit the server with CONTROL-C.
```

Now you can open a web browser and visit *http://localhost:8000/* and see the demonstration app! The app lets you create simple messages (optionally with attached images) which are persisted in MongoDB.

Let us examine how the sample app works. Take a look at the file `status/view.py`. This is where the MongoDB connection is created, and where most of the application logic is stored. In their Django + MongoDB integration example, 10gen take a different approach from the others outlined in this chapter. They create a PyMongo `Database` in the global scope of the views module, rather than attaching it to request objects as in Pyramid or making it a framework-wide global as in Pylons 1.x:

```
import datetime
import string
import random
import mimetypes
import cStringIO as StringIO

from PIL import Image
from django.http import HttpResponse
from django.http import HttpResponseRedirect
from django.shortcuts import render_to_response
from pymongo.connection import Connection
from pymongo import DESCENDING
import gridfs

db = Connection().sms
```

This approach is simple and works fine for a demo. However, in larger Django projects with multiple installed applications (in this sample, there is a single installed app—it is named "status") this would require a separate PyMongo connection pool to be maintained for each app. This results in wasted MongoDB connections and duplicated code. Instead, it would be recommended to create the connection in a single place and import it in any other modules which need access.

This should be enough information to get you started building your Django MongoDB application.

Going Further

In this book we have tried to give you a solid grasp of how to leverage MongoDB in real-world applications. You should have a decent understanding of how to go about modeling your data, writing effective queries and avoiding concurrency problems such as race conditions and deadlocks. There are a number of other advanced topics which we didn't have space for in this book but are nonetheless worth looking into as you build your application. Notably, map-reduce enables computing aggregates efficiently. Sharding permits you to scale your application beyond the available memory of a single machine. GridFS allows you to store binary data in MongoDB. Capped Collections are a special type of collection, which look like a circular buffer and are great for log data. With these features at your disposal, Python and MongoDB are extremely powerful tools to have in your toolbox when developing an application.

About the Author

Niall O'Higgins is a software consultant specializing in mobile, tablet, and cloud computing. His accomplishments include designing and implementing the Catch.com platform backend using MongoDB, Python, and Pylons. Catch is one of the most popular apps on Android. Prior to Catch, he was a software engineer at Metaweb Technologies, where he worked on Freebase.com (now owned by Google). He is the founder and organizer of both the San Francisco Python Web Technology Meet-up, PyWebSF, and the Bay Area Tablet Computing Group, We Have Tablets. He has published quite a bit of Open Source software—contributing to OpenBSD among others—and frequently speaks at conferences and events. You can find him on Twitter as @niallohiggins.

Get even more for your money.

Join the O'Reilly Community, and register the O'Reilly books you own. It's free, and you'll get:

- $4.99 ebook upgrade offer
- 40% upgrade offer on O'Reilly print books
- Membership discounts on books and events
- Free lifetime updates to ebooks and videos
- Multiple ebook formats, DRM FREE
- Participation in the O'Reilly community
- Newsletters
- Account management
- 100% Satisfaction Guarantee

Signing up is easy:

1. **Go to: oreilly.com/go/register**
2. **Create an O'Reilly login.**
3. **Provide your address.**
4. **Register your books.**

Note: English-language books only

To order books online:
oreilly.com/store

For questions about products or an order:
orders@oreilly.com

To sign up to get topic-specific email announcements and/or news about upcoming books, conferences, special offers, and new technologies:
elists@oreilly.com

For technical questions about book content:
booktech@oreilly.com

To submit new book proposals to our editors:
proposals@oreilly.com

O'Reilly books are available in multiple DRM-free ebook formats. For more information:
oreilly.com/ebooks

O'REILLY®

The information you need, when and where you need it.

With Safari Books Online, you can:

Access the contents of thousands of technology and business books

- Quickly search over 7000 books and certification guides
- Download whole books or chapters in PDF format, at no extra cost, to print or read on the go
- Copy and paste code
- Save up to 35% on O'Reilly print books
- **New!** Access mobile-friendly books directly from cell phones and mobile devices

Stay up-to-date on emerging topics before the books are published

- Get on-demand access to evolving manuscripts.
- Interact directly with authors of upcoming books

Explore thousands of hours of video on technology and design topics

- Learn from expert video tutorials
- Watch and replay recorded conference sessions

O'REILLY®